# Learning the Notes on the Violin, Book Two: The D-String Book

### By Cassia Harvey

(Formerly *The D-String Book for Violin*)

CHP425

©2022 by C. Harvey Publications  All Rights Reserved.

www.charveypublications.com - print books
www.learnstrings.com - PDF downloadable books
www.harveystringarrangements.com - chamber music

## Table of Contents

| Section | Page |
|---|---|
| Reading Notes | 4 |
| Parts of the Staff | 5 |
| Time Signatures Used | 6 |
| How Time Signatures Work | 6 |
| Rhythm: Notes and Rests Used | 7 |
| The Notes Learned in the Book | 8 |
| Another Way of Seeing the Notes | 9 |
| Open D | 10 |
| Open D and First Finger E | 12 |
| Open D, First Finger E, and Second Finger F-sharp | 16 |
| Open D, First Finger E, Second Finger F-sharp, and Third Finger G | 25 |
| Open D, First Finger E, Second Finger F-sharp, Third Finger G, and Fourth Finger A | 34 |

## Reading Notes

This book gives struggling note-readers a chance to focus on and learn the notes on the D string. This book can be studied on its own or—even better—along with the other books in this series.

While it is possible to play the violin without being able to read notes, you will need to be able to read notes to play most classical violin repertoire or with others in a chamber group or orchestra. Some of the most enjoyable violin playing requires music reading simply because there are too many notes to learn by rote and remember!

Since **the best thing you can do to improve your note-reading is to play a lot of different music at the same level** (kind of like immersing yourself in a language), check out some of the other Level 0 books listed at the end of this book and see which ones can work for you.

## Writing Notes in this Book

It is perfectly acceptable to write in a music book like this one, however tradition dictates that we can **only write on music with pencil**; never with anything permanent like pen or marker.

As you write the notes, use the drawing process to help you recognize and remember the notes in the exercises and pieces that follow. **Try to remember where the notehead (the oval part of the note) of each note sits on the staff and how it looks,** so that you can match that with the note letter name and the finger number you will use to play it.

©2022 C. Harvey Publications® All Rights Reserved.

Learning the Notes on the Violin, Book Two, the D-String Book

## Parts of the Staff

**Clef:** Unlike some other instruments, the violin only reads one clef: treble clef (also called G clef.)

**Staff:** We read notes by seeing where the note-heads are placed on the lines and spaces of staff.

**Line note:** The line slices right through the middle of the note.

**Space note:** Sits in between two lines.

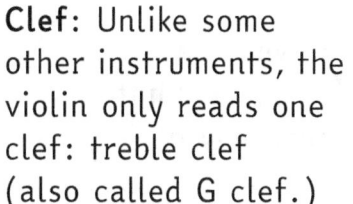

**Time Signature:** This tells you how many beats are in each measure and how to count the beats.

**Barline:** Music is broken up into measures, separated by vertical lines, called barlines.

**Double Bar:** A thick double line tells you it is the end of the piece.

**Key Signature:** The sharps or flats at the beginning of each line tell you which notes to raise or lower in the piece.

**Stem:** The stem (the line next to the note-head on some notes) can go up or down but doesn't affect the name of the note. Both of these notes have the same name (B) even though the stems go in different directions.

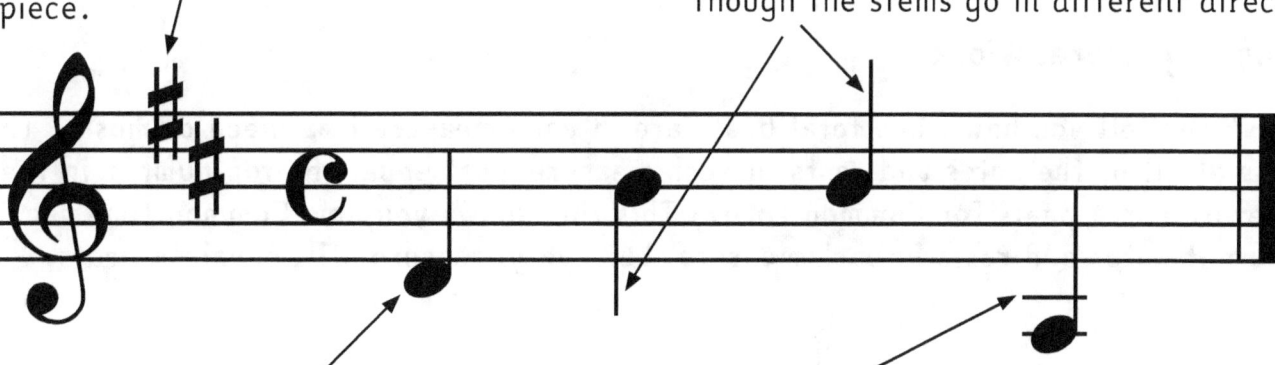

**Note-head:** The note-head is the dot or circle that is the most important part of learning the note name. The line or space where the note-head sits tells you the name of the note.

**Ledger line:** To help readability, notes above or below the staff have ledger lines, which are extra lines that help you see where the notes fit in relation to the staff.

©2022 C. Harvey Publications® All Rights Reserved.

## Time Signatures Used in this Book

C means "Common time," which tells you that there are 4 beats in a measure and a quarter note gets one beat. Common time is another way of writing 4.
           4

3  timing tells you that there are
4    3 beats in a measure and that a quarter note gets one beat.

2  timing tells you that there are
4    2 beats in a measure and that a quarter note gets one beat.

6  timing tells you that there are
8    6 beats in a measure and that an eighth note gets one beat.

## How Time Signatures Work

Time signatures tell you how many total beats are in each measure in a piece of music. The total beats of all of the notes and rests in each measure must equal the top number in the time signature (or 4 beats for Common time.) This line shows you how Common time can have different notes and rests in each measure, but every measure still equals 4 beats.

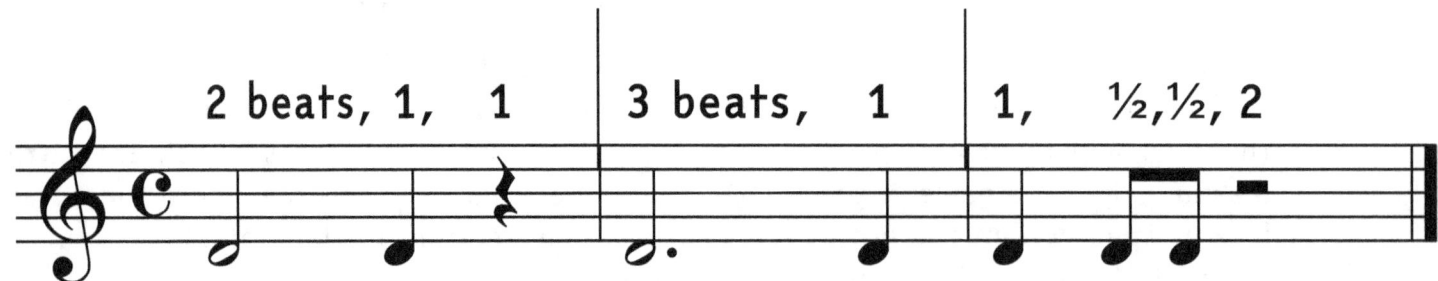

## Rhythm: The Main Note and Rests Used in this Book

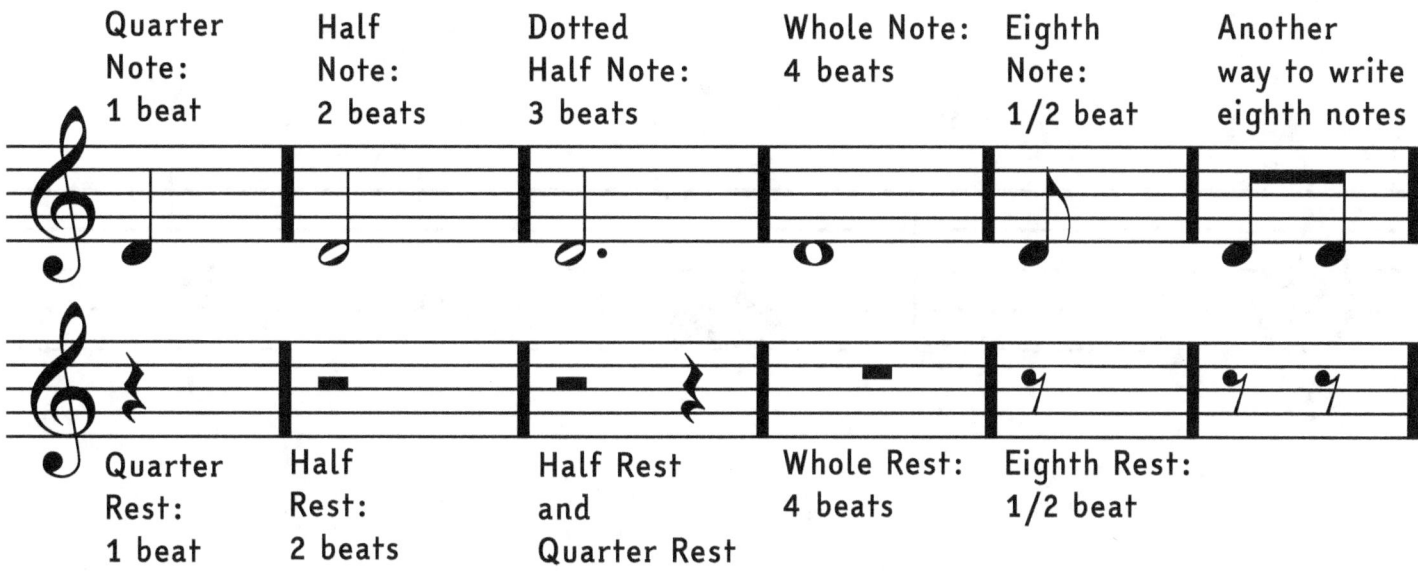

## How the Notes Relate to Each Other

## 6/8 Rhythm: A different way of thinking!

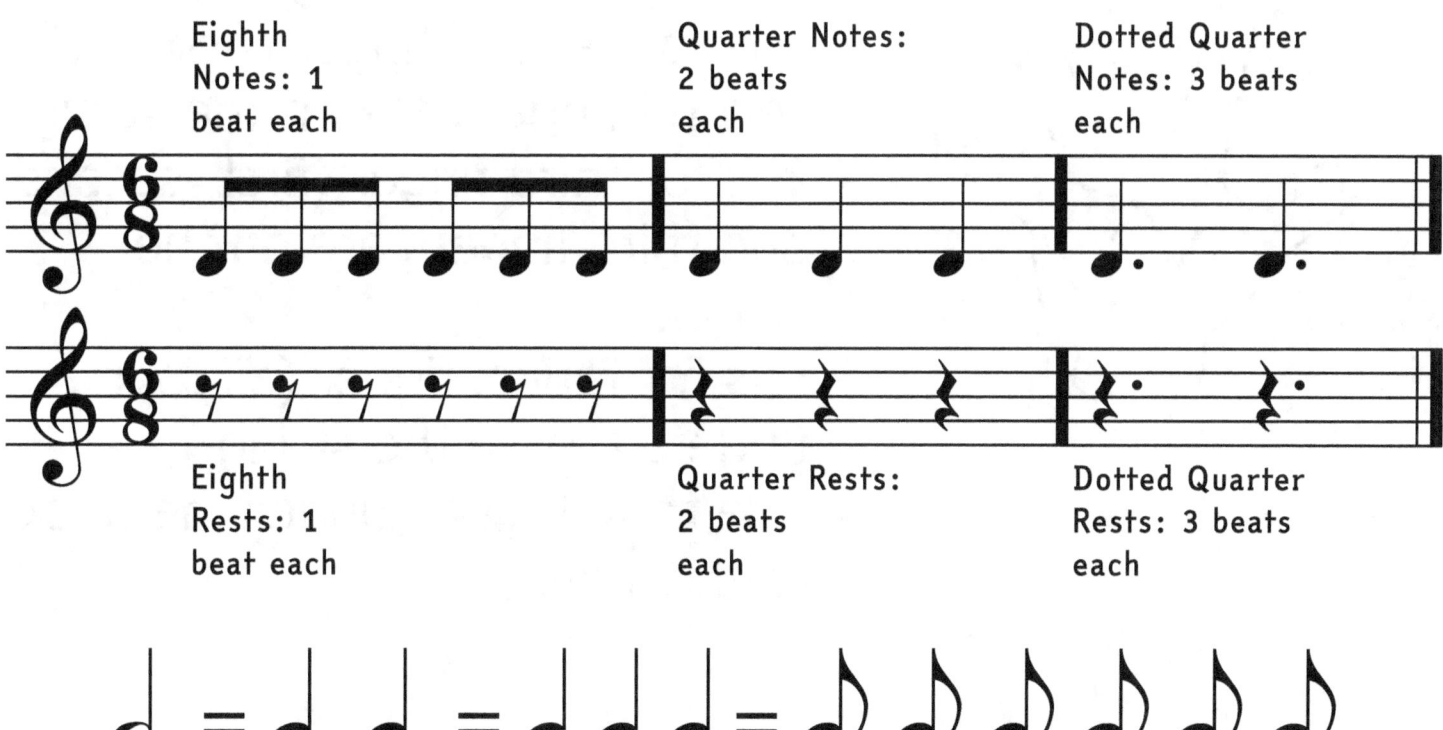

## The Notes Learned in this Book

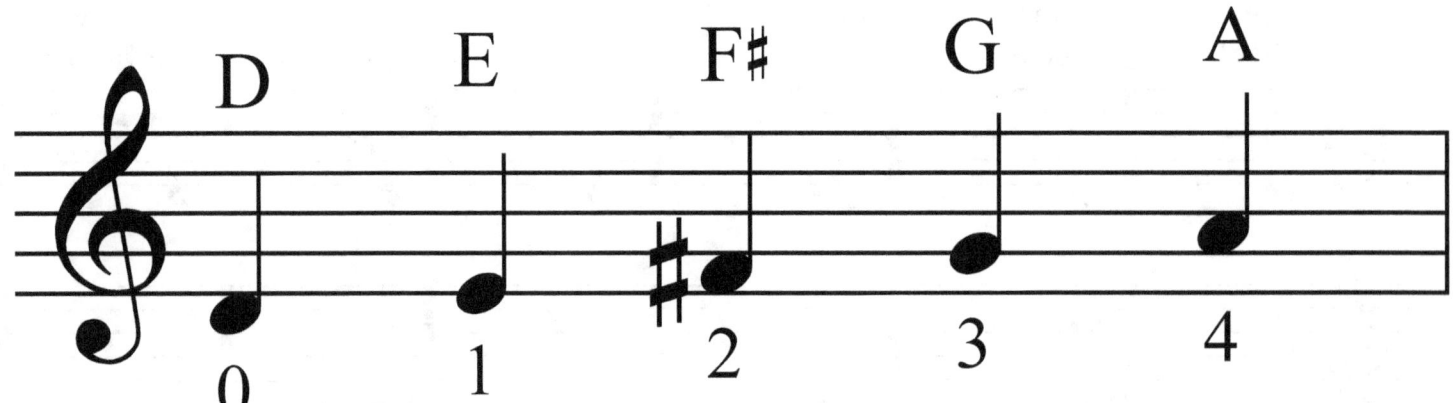

## How Finger Numbers Work

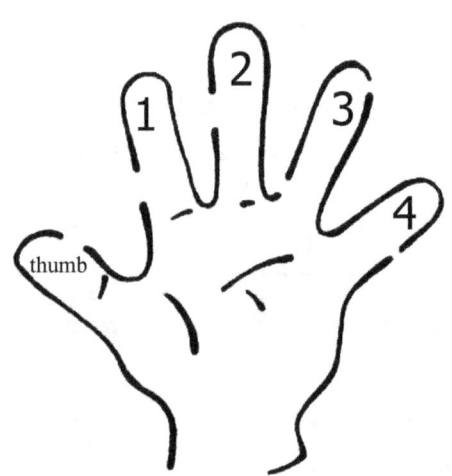

- 0 is for open string (no fingers are on the string.)
- 1 is for first finger (first finger only is on the string.)
- 2 is for second finger (first and second fingers are on the string.)
- 3 is for third finger (first, second, and third fingers are on the string.)
- 4 is for fourth finger (all four fingers are on the string.)
- The thumb goes under the neck of the violin.

# Another Way of Seeing the Notes

Hold your violin and look at how the notes match your fingers as you play them.

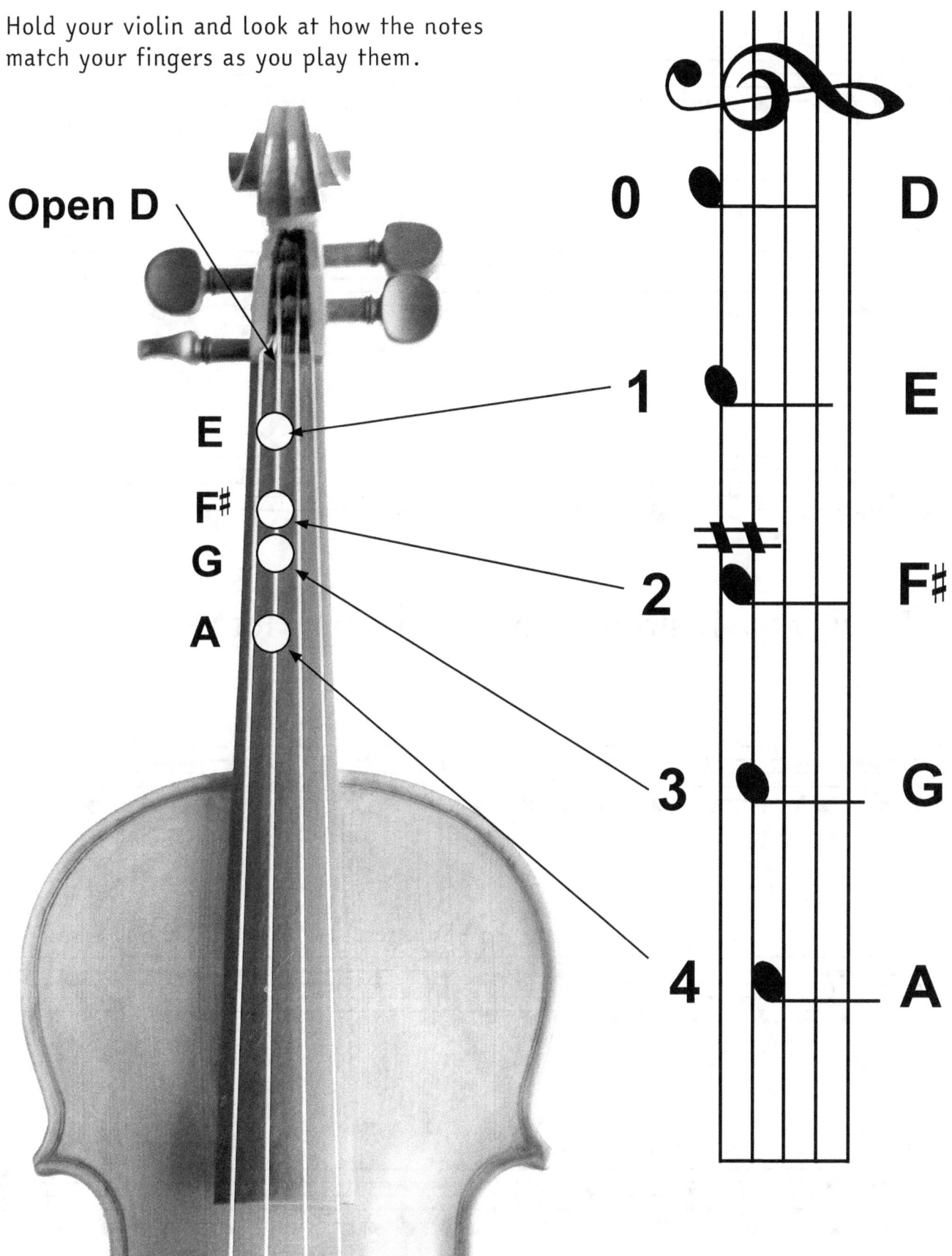

## Playing the D string

Cassia Harvey

## Playing the D string with "Mississippi Hot Dog"

## Writing the Note "D"

Write four "D" quarter notes.

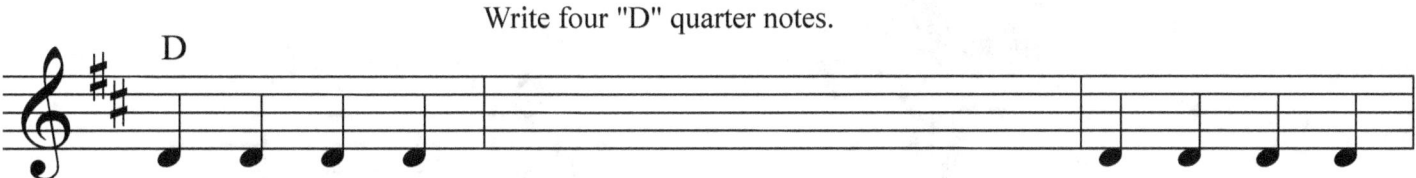

Write four "D" quarter notes.    Write four "D" quarter notes.

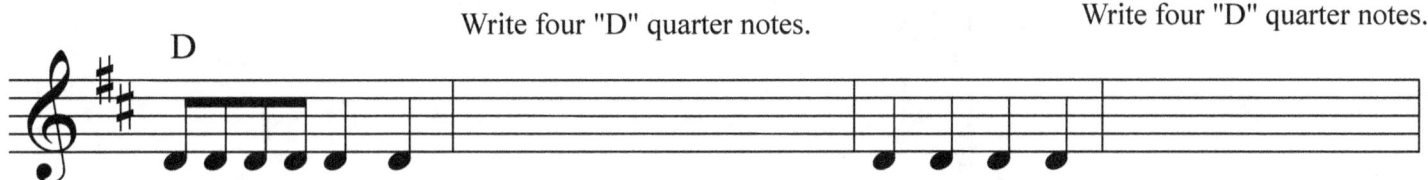

Write four "D" quarter notes.

## Rhythm Review

## First Finger "E" on the D String

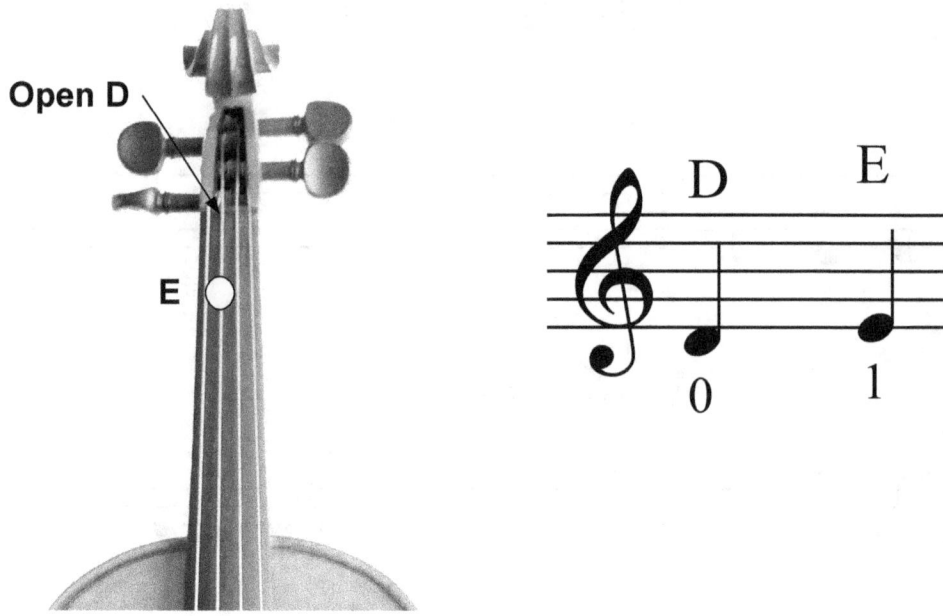

Write the note names below the notes.

Draw the notes played by each finger number on the D string and write their names under the notes.

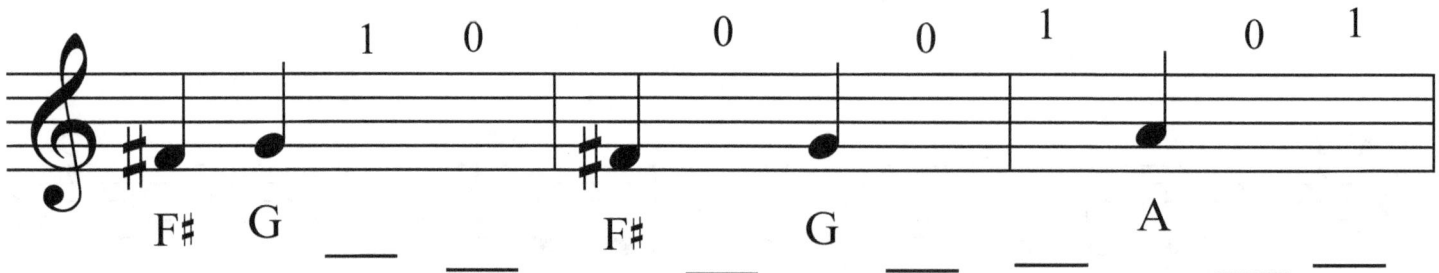

## First Finger "E" on the D String

## Rhythms with D and E

## D String March

## Reviewing the Note "E"

©2022 C. Harvey Publications® All Rights Reserved.

## Fiddling on the High Seas

## First Finger Jive

## Second Finger "F#" on the D String

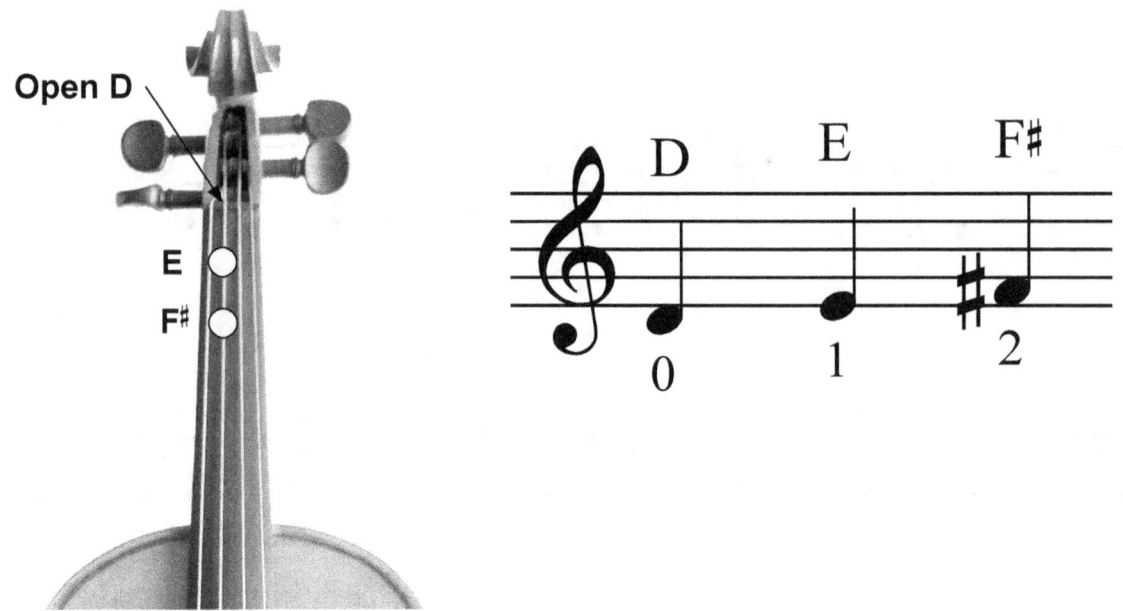

Write the note names below the notes.

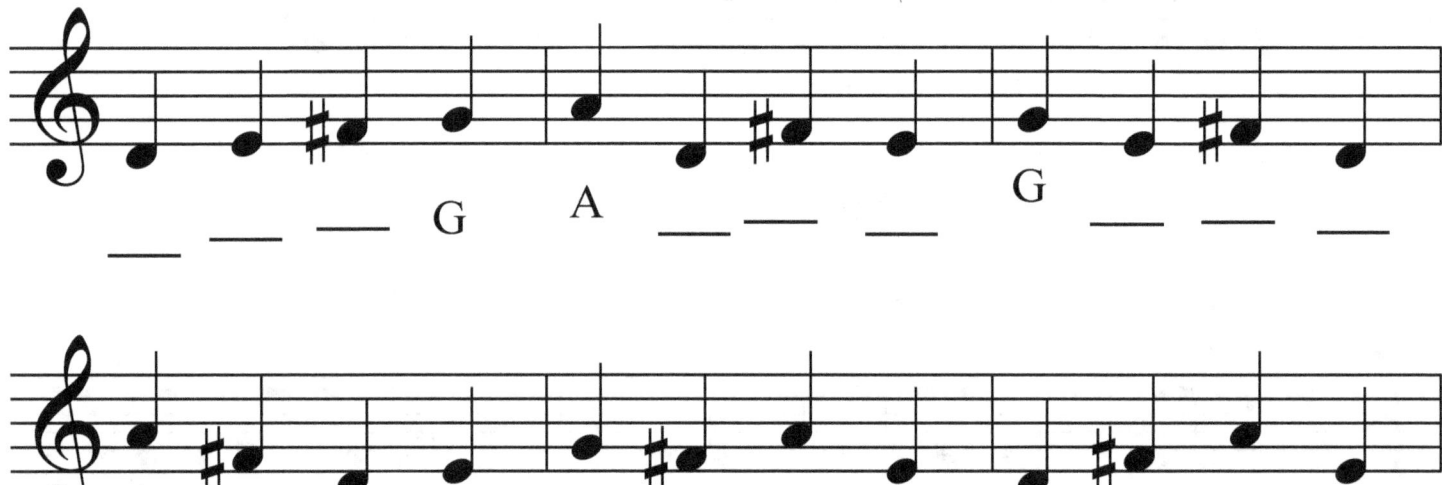

Draw the notes played by each finger number on the D string and write their names under the notes.

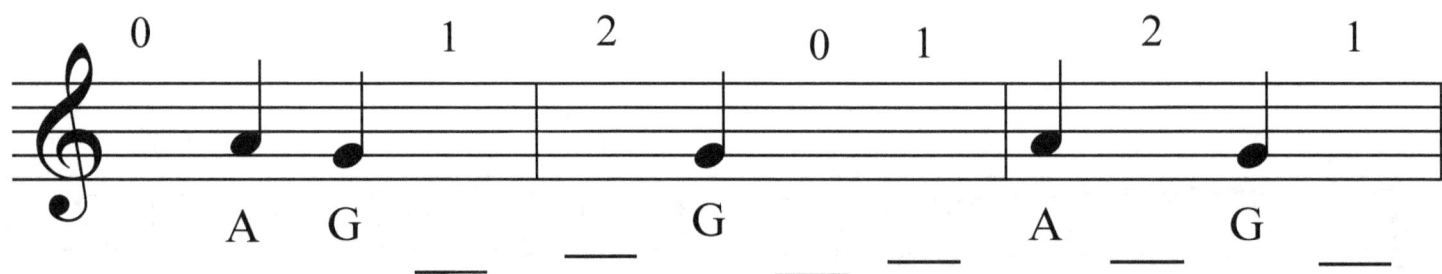

## Learning Second Finger "F#"

## Mary Had a Little Lamb

## Hot Cross Buns with Variations

## Squashed Bread

American Folk Tune

©2022 C. Harvey Publications® All Rights Reserved.

# Note-Name Study #1

D E D E

F# E F# E

D E F# E

D F# E D

# Note-Name Study #2

F# D E F#

E D E D

F# D E F#

E F# E D

## The Coordination Song

## Running To the Waves

## Jellyfish

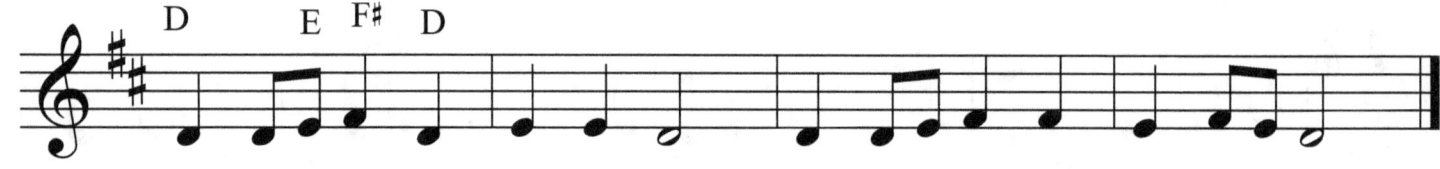

©2022 C. Harvey Publications® All Rights Reserved.

# Worksheet Page

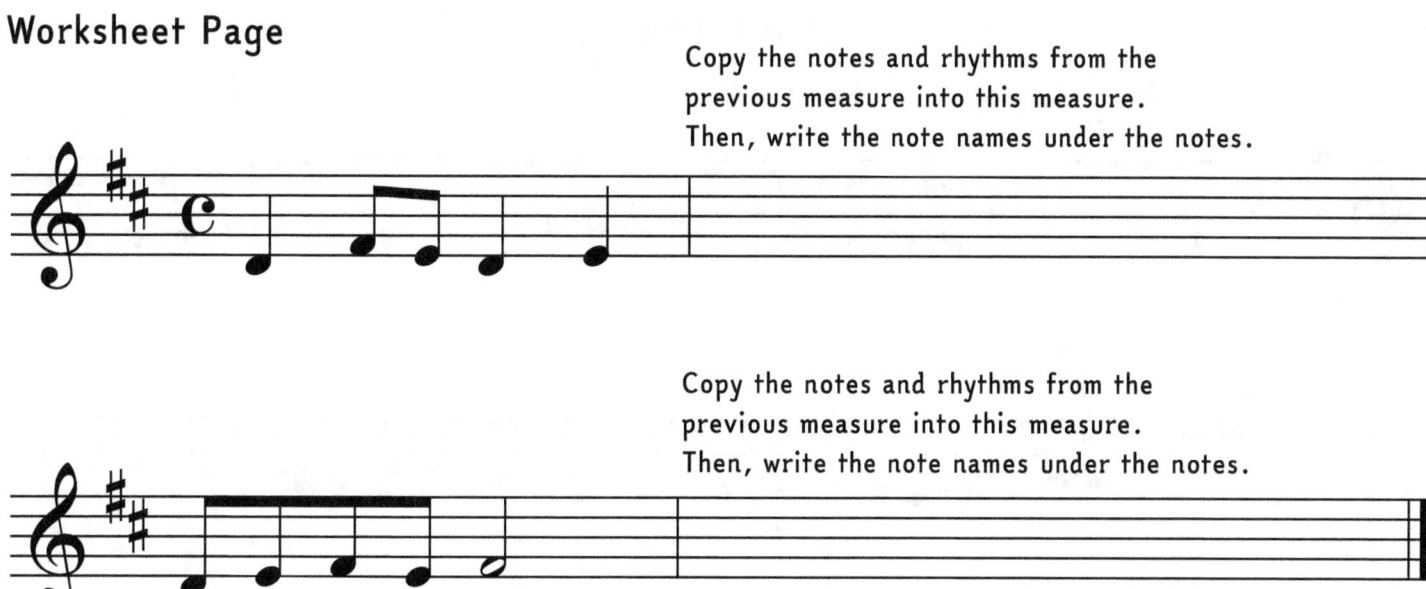

Copy the notes and rhythms from the previous measure into this measure.
Then, write the note names under the notes.

Copy the notes and rhythms from the previous measure into this measure.
Then, write the note names under the notes.

Draw the barlines in each piece to match the time signature. Then, write the finger numbers over the notes and the note names under the notes.

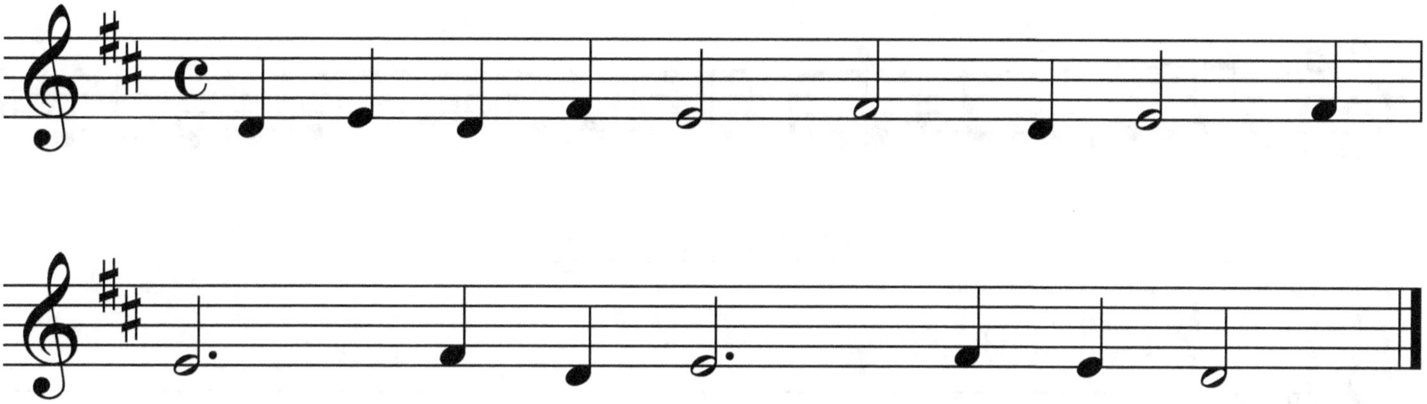

## Finger Trainer

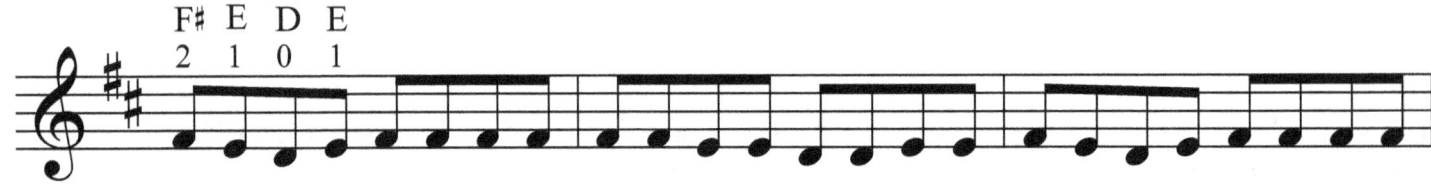

## Dolphin Song

Make your bows as smooth as possible.

©2022 C. Harvey Publications® All Rights Reserved.

## Skipping to Second Finger

## Straight to the Moon

French Folk Song

## Taking a Boat Ride

## Seasick

# Third Finger "G" on the D String

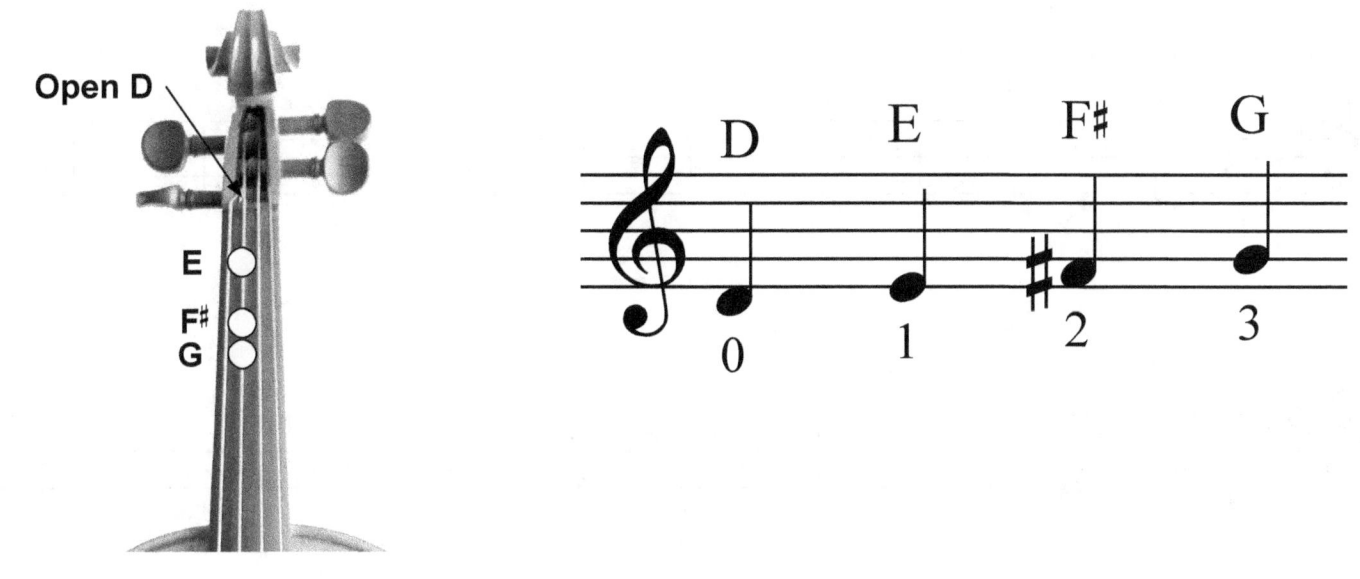

Write the note names below the notes.

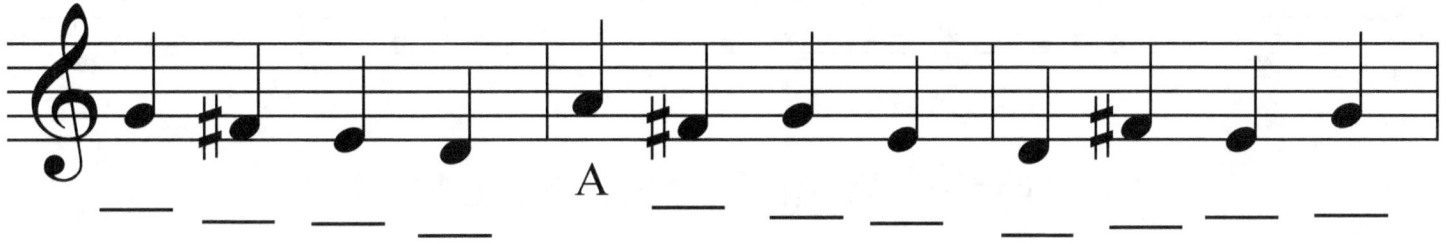

Draw the notes played by each finger number on the D string and write their names under the notes.

## Learning 3rd Finger "G"

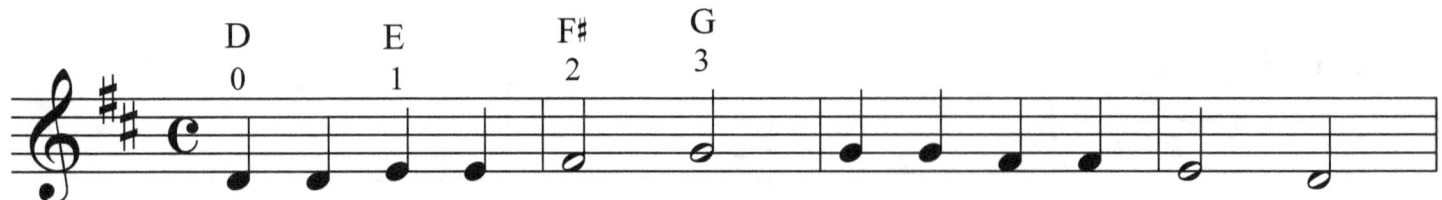

## Rhythm With the New Note "G"

## Searching for Pennies in the Sand

## The Skipping Study

©2022 C. Harvey Publications® All Rights Reserved.

## The Scale Workout

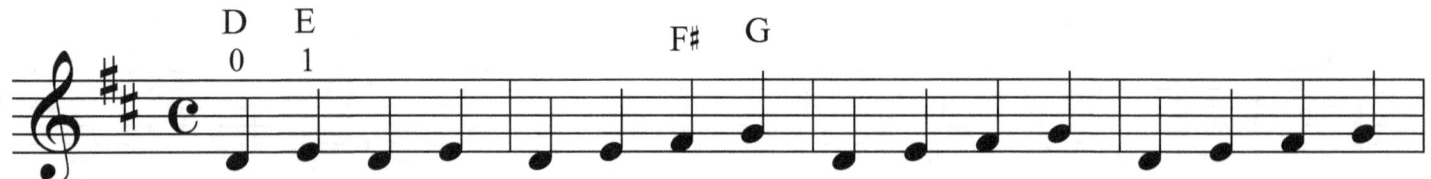

## Little French Song

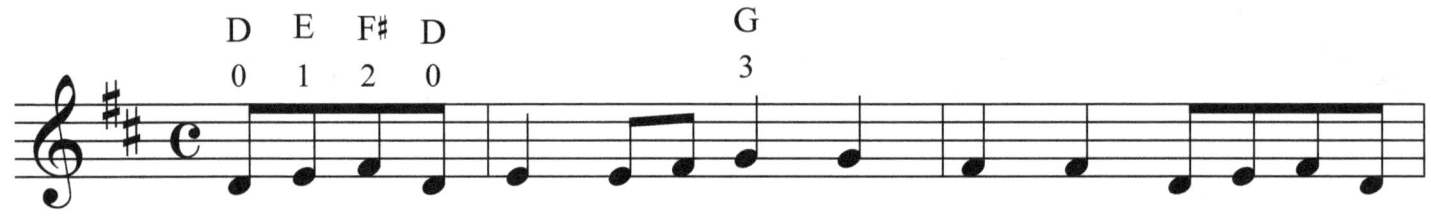

©2022 C. Harvey Publications® All Rights Reserved.

Learning the Notes on the Violin, Book Two, the D-String Book

# Worksheet Page

Copy the notes and rhythms from the previous measure into this measure.
Then, write the note names under the notes.

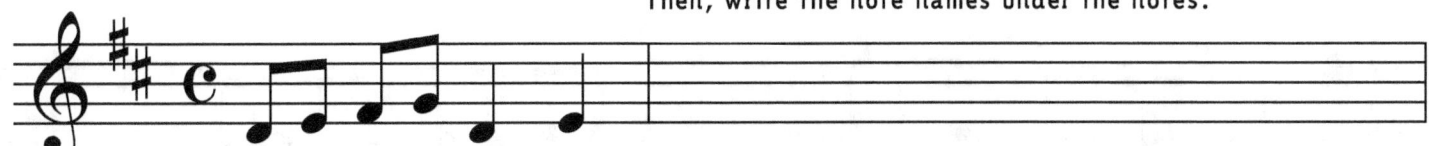

Copy the notes and rhythms from the previous measure into this measure.
Then, write the note names under the notes.

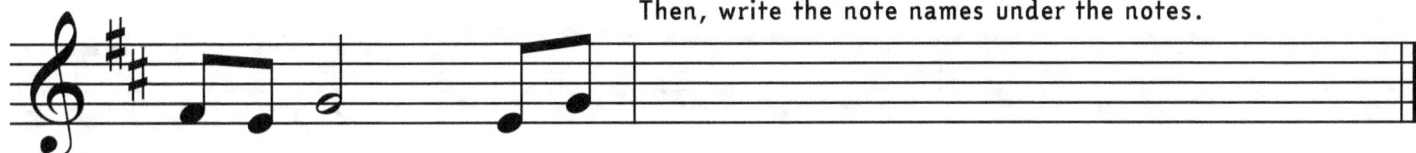

Draw the barlines in each piece to match the time signature. Then, write the finger numbers over the notes and the note names under the notes.

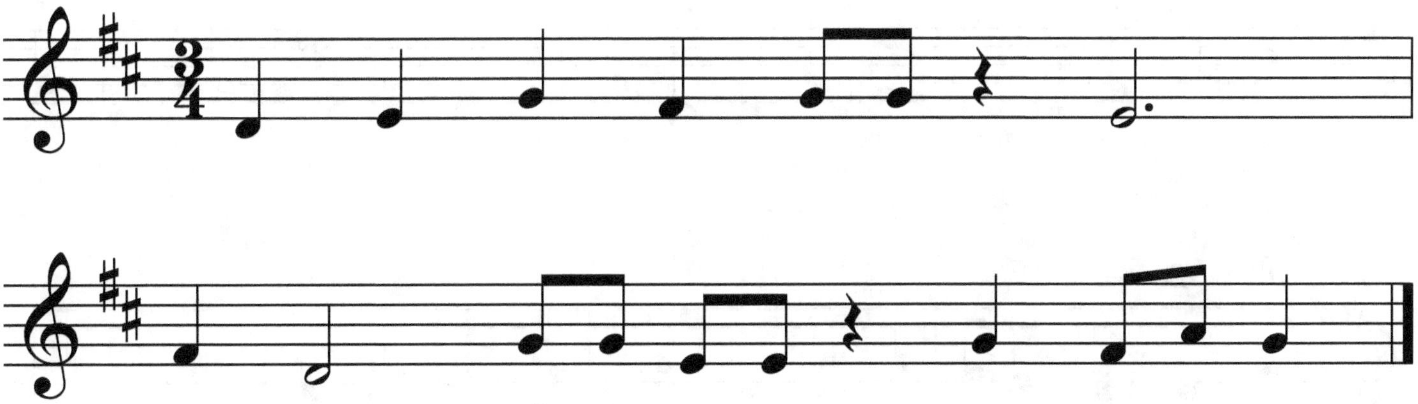

©2022 C. Harvey Publications® All Rights Reserved.

## D String Exercise

## Danish Contredans

## The Sandal Song

Folk Song

## Counting Exercise

## Wild Horse Rhythm Training

Here, a quarter note gets 2 counts!

## The Wild Horses

## Fourth Finger "A" on the D String

Write the note names below the notes.

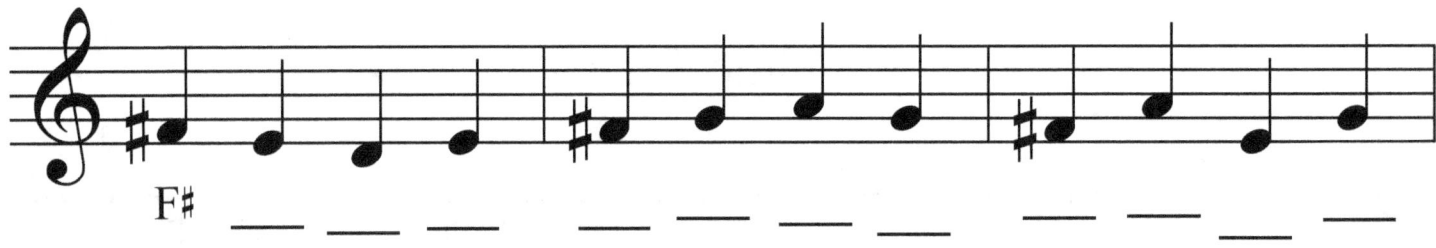

F# ___  ___  ___  ___  ___  ___  ___  ___  ___  ___  ___

___  ___  ___  ___  ___  ___  ___  ___  ___  ___  ___

Draw the notes played by each finger number on the D string and write their names under the notes.

D ___  ___  ___  ___  ___  ___  ___  ___  ___  ___

## Learning 4th Finger "A"

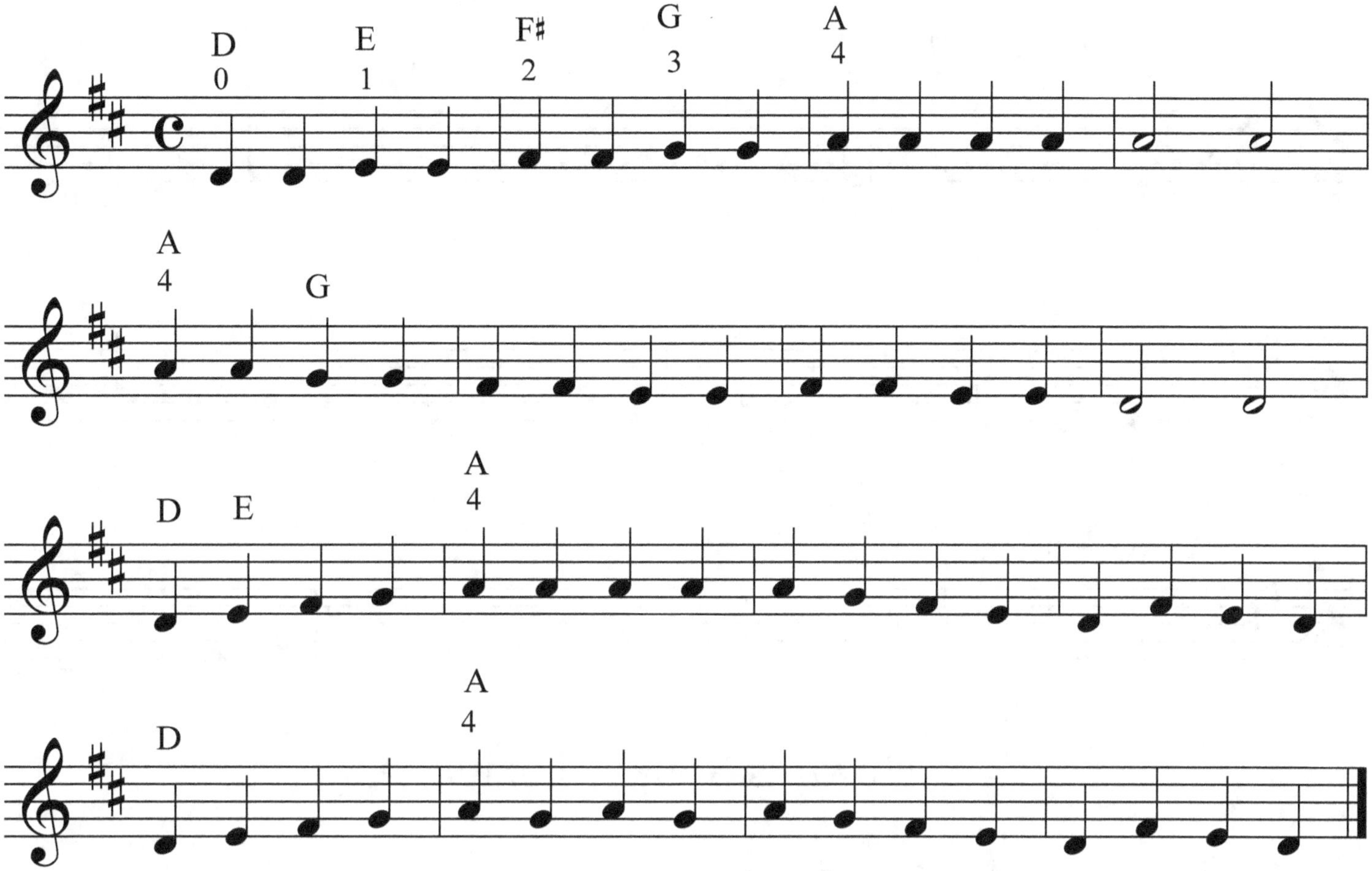

## John Peel

English Folk Song

©2022 C. Harvey Publications® All Rights Reserved.

## Using Fourth Finger "A"

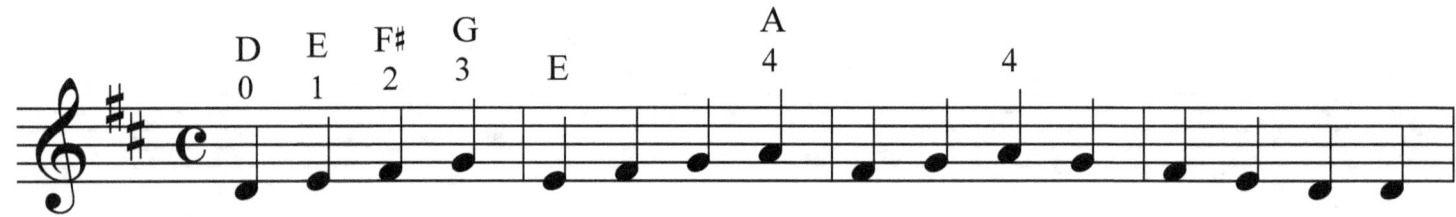

## Mozart's Sonata Theme

# Skipping Exercise

## Shoemaker's Dance
Danish Folk Song

## Worksheet Page

Copy the notes and rhythms from the previous measure into this measure.
Then, write the note names under the notes.

Copy the notes and rhythms from the previous measure into this measure.
Then, write the note names under the notes.

Draw the barlines in each piece to match the time signature. Then, write the finger numbers over the notes and the note names under the notes.

©2022 C. Harvey Publications® All Rights Reserved.

# More Counting in 6/8

Here, a quarter note gets 2 counts!

## Humpty Dumpty

English Folk Song

## The Speed Exercise

## Folk Lullaby

German Folk Song

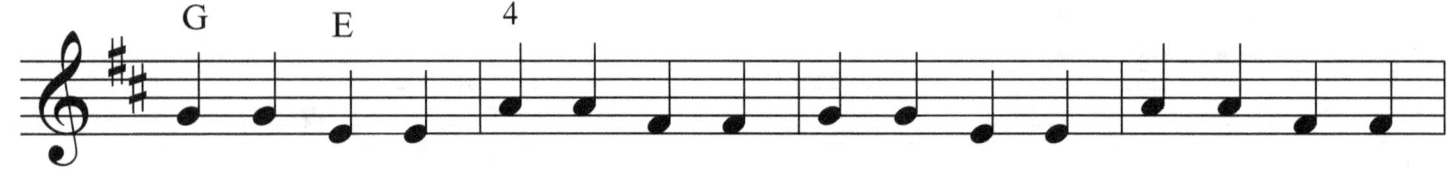

# Learning the Notes on the Violin, Book Two, the D-String Book

**Each measure below uses one of these time signatures:** 4/4 or 3/4 or 2/4

**Write the time signature in at the beginning of each measure, then write the note name below each note and the finger number above each note.**

## Finger Twister

## The Galloping Pony

American Folk Song

# Warm-Up #1

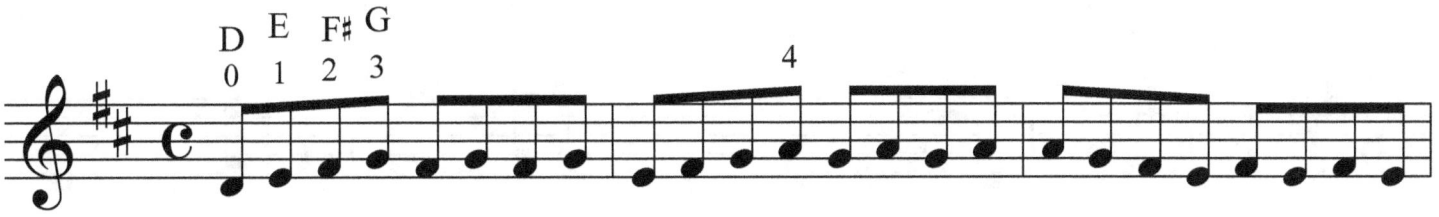

## Little Sally Waters

English Folk Song

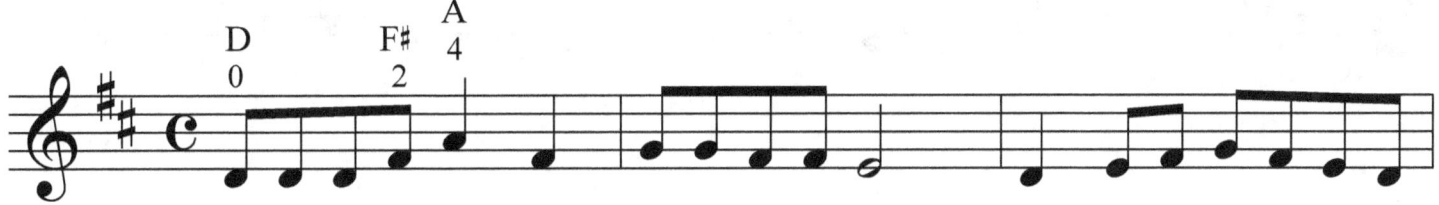

## Note Review

## Yankee Doodle

American Folk Song

Learning the Notes on the Violin, Book Two, the D-String Book 45

# Rhythm Answers

Page 41 Time Signature Answers

Page 38 Barline Answers

Page 29 Barline Answers

Page 21 Barline Answers

©2022 C. Harvey Publications® All Rights Reserved.

# The Books in this Series

Learning the Notes on the Violin, Book One, the A-String Book CHP424
Learning the Notes on the Violin, Book Two, the D-String Book CHP425
Learning the Notes on the Violin, Book Three, the G-String Book CHP426
Learning the Notes on the Violin, Book Four, the E-String Book CHP427

# Other Books Around this Level

**The Open-String Book for Violin**
Short open-string studies for the beginning violinist. CHP249 $9

**The Hot Cross Buns Book for Violin**
50 variations on Hot Cross Buns for the beginning violinist. CHP154 $9

**Learning the Violin, Book One**
A fun, stress-free method for individual learning or string classes. CHP280 $9

**The 'Mary Had a Little Lamb' Book for Violin**
50 variations on Mary Had a Little Lamb for the beginning violinist. CHP168 $9

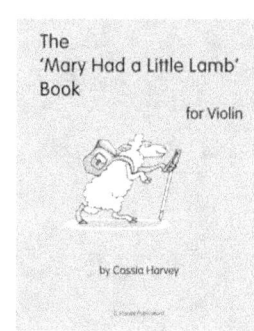

**Early Exercises for the Violin**
Very easy exercises for beginning violinists.
CHP292 $9

All print books are available from www.charveypublications.com, on online retail sites, or through your local music store.

Some books are available as PDF downloadable books on www.learnstrings.com.

www.ingramcontent.com/pod-product-compliance
Lightning Source LLC
Chambersburg PA
CBHW081409070526
44583CB00020B/2740